GREAT EXPERIMENTS *with*

H_2O

Noel Fiarotta & Phyllis Fiarotta

Sterling Publishing Co., Inc.
New York

Dedicated to Beth Anderson, Patty Yoemans, and all physically challenged children, who stand, every day, as tall as the mighty spruce, and to Jimmy McGrath, senior water repairman, Jersey City Water Department, N.J.

Edited by Jeanette Green

1 3 5 7 9 10 8 6 4 2

Published in 1997 by Sterling Publishing Company, Inc.
387 Park Avenue South, New York, N.Y. 10016
Originally published in hard cover as *Water Science, Water Fun*
© 1996 by Noel Fiarotta & Phyllis Fiarotta
Distributed in Canada by Sterling Publishing
% Canadian Manda Group, One Atlantic Avenue, Suite 105
Toronto, Ontario, Canada M6K 3E7
Distributed in Great Britain and Europe by Cassell PLC
Wellington House, 125 Strand, London WC2R 0BB, England
Distributed in Australia by Capricorn Link (Australia) Pty Ltd.
P.O. Box 6651, Baulkham Hills, Business Centre, NSW 2153, Australia
Printed in Hong Kong
All rights reserved

Sterling ISBN 0-8069-4249-5

CONTENTS

A Brief History 6

What Is Water? 10

Water Is a Liquid at Rest 11
Water's Many Uses 12
Cohesion *Bulging Water* 13
Surface Tension *Magic Floats* 14
Floating *Apple Bobbing* 15
Dispersion *Holes in Water* 16
Leaching *Sun Tea* 17
Solvent *Rainbow Garden* 18
Saturation *Rock Candy* 19
Density *Submarine Egg* 20
Sound *Glass Chimes* 21
Refraction *Bent Beam* 22
Magnification *Magnifying Glass* 23
Displacement *Sink Like a Rock* 24
Temperature *Cold Water Sinks* 25
Seepage *Marbleized Eggs* 26
Reconstitution *Blow-up Fruit* 27
Roots *Windowsill Garden* 28
Germination *Bean Sprouts* 29
Habitat *Painted Fishbowl* 30

Water Is a Liquid in Motion 31
The Journey of Water 32
Gravity *Level* 34
Agitation *Snow Globe* 35
Vortex *Glittering Whirlpool* 36
Solution *Tart & Sweet* 37
Emulsion *Separation* 38
Pressure *Against Gravity* 39
Heat *Underwater Eruption* 40
Currents *Game in a Jar* 41
Absorption *Disappear Like Magic* 42
Buoyancy *Sailboat Race* 43
Ripples & Reflections *Rock Skipping* 44
Dripping *Water Clock* 45
Raindrops *Droplet Painting* 46
Fluidity *Quill Pen* 47
Stream *Water Slide* 48
Diversion *Water Pipes* 49
Siphoning *Leap Frog* 50
Weight *Water Spouts* 51
Energy *Waterwheel* 52
Spreading *Water Blots* 53
Bleeding *Tee-Shirt* 54

Capillarity   *Tinted Celery*   55
Rejuvenation   *Thirsty Plants*   56

Water Is a Solid, Crystal & Vapor   57

Water's Other Personalities   58
Freezing   *Growing Water*   59
Inclusions   *Punch Ice*   60
Melting   *Pressure & Salt*   61
Sliding   *Summer Hockey*   62
Fractures   *Snow Cone*   63
Formation   *Icicles*   64
Heat Energy   *Freezing Rate*   65
Refrigeration   *Ice Cream*   66
Frost   *Jack Frost*   67

Ice Crystals   *Snowflake Catcher*   68
Adhesion   *Rolled Snow Animals*   69
Molding & Compacting
        Building Blocks   70
Volume   *Precipitation Gauge*   71
Condensation   *Iced Beverage*   72
Transpiration   *Recycling*   73
Suction   *Suspended Spoon*   74
Mist   *Rainbow*   75
Steam   *Haunted House*   76
Fragrance   *Simmering Potpourri*   77
Evaporation   *Croutons*   78

Water Smarts   79
Index   80

Fun.

Serious.

Mysterious.

It has no taste.

It has no fragrance.

It does not have color. You
can sink or swim in it. You can slip
and slide on it. It is home to a starfish family.
Clouds of it play with night stars. It flutters from the
sky as ice crystals. It accumulates on grass as morning dew.
At dawn and on high mountains it becomes mist. It covers two-
thirds of the earth. It noisily rattles rooftops during blustery weather and quietly disappears from a glass exposed to air. It pro-
vides energy. It allows travel and invites recreation. And for
all plants and all creatures of our planet, it is necessary
for existence. Water, water, water, water.

A BRIEF HISTORY

WATER'S BEGINNINGS

Scientists believe that the universe began with a big explosion, which they call the big bang. Gases, hurled into space, eventually became galaxies made up of countless suns and planets.

Earth was first a ball of fire. Steam and gases, rising into the upper atmosphere, cooled and turned into a kind of rain.

The rain returned to steam when it hit the planet's surface. This repetition cooled earth and left behind the great seas.

Life began in the seas, first as one-celled organisms. Eventually a fishlike creature, able to breath air, crawled out of the water and lived on land. For hundreds of millions of years, life took many forms, from the tiny snail to the dinosaurs, some of which were the largest creatures to roam the earth.

BY THE WATER'S EDGE

Many early people lived in caves. In search of food, hunters sometimes wandered long distances to lakes and streams. Not only was fresh water a source of fish, but it attracted animals which came there to drink and feed.

People gradually began to build shelters along the shores of rivers and lakes, which provided them food and fresh drinking water. Soon a few dwellings grew into a small community, which grew into a village.

As the population increased, people required more food than the rivers and lakes could provide. People learned to farm. And they used fresh water to **irrigate** the crops they planted along the water's edge. They also domesticated animals.

WATER MANAGEMENT

Once people learned to collect water, they were no longer as dependent on rivers or lakes and could build settlements further away. In ancient villages and towns, large stone tubs called **cisterns** caught and stored rainwater for drinking.

People eventually realized that water flowed underground and that there were fresh water **springs.** Large holes were dug where water was thought to be. People brought the water from the depths with buckets attached to ropes. And these water **wells** suppled drinking water for people in towns.

The ancient Romans invented the **arch** which allowed them to build long, stone **aqueducts** across great distances. The aqueducts channeled water from the lakes and streams to towns and cities.

WATER FOR TRAVEL

When people added sails to their boats, they used the wind to travel faster and further. Explorers from different countries crossed large bodies of water to visit foreign lands.

Boats carried passengers and goods from one port to another, which seemed to make the world a smaller place. Sailors told folktales of fabulous creatures, mermaids, and sea serpents. But whales, porpoises, manatees, and optical effects usually inspired these tall tales.

Today we enjoy our ponds, lakes, rivers, and oceans, as well as swimming pools, for recreation and sports, such as canoeing, fishing, sailing, diving, waterskiing, and swimming.

WHAT IS WATER?

Matter is what all things are made of. **Gas** is matter that is neither liquid nor solid. When the gases oxygen, hydrogen, and carbon dioxide combine in a certain proportion, they remain gases in a mixture we call air. When two parts **hydrogen** and one part **oxygen** combine, they change from gases into a **liquid** called water. The **chemical formula** for water is H_2O.

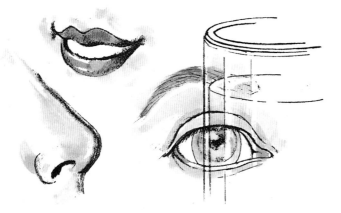

Water is a liquid that is tasteless, odorless, colorless, and transparent. The nature of water changes when you add other substances to it. If you stir in raspberry pulp, water will taste like raspberries. Add lemon juice, it will smell like lemon. A crushed cranberry adds pink color, and black ink makes water no longer transparent. Amazingly, water has many other personalities, which you are about to discover.

WATER IS A LIQUID
AT REST

WATER'S MANY USES

A **liquid** is a substance that **flows** easily, like water. But water does not always flow. Standing water can be found in a puddle after a rainstorm, in a birdbath for feathered friends, and in a cool, refreshing swimming pool.

People, as well as animals, use water for cleansing. We use it to brush our teeth, wash our hands, and clean our clothes. And let's not forget a tub filled with bubble bath.

A lake, a large body of standing water, is home to many animals. Ducks live on the lake, frogs and fish live in the lake, and deer and bears drink at the water's edge.

People enjoy lakes for boating, swimming, and fishing. Sometimes lakes are **reservoirs** for fresh drinking water.

12

COHESION

All substances are made up of **molecules.** Molecules are tiny particles that are attracted to each other. **Cohesion** is the attraction (sticking together) of molecules. On the surface of water, cohesion forms a kind of rubbery "skin."

BULGING WATER

CHECKLIST   drinking glass • dish • water • spoon

1. Place a drinking glass filled with water on a dish.
2. Study the rim of the glass at eye level while you slowly spoon in small amounts of water.

RESULT   The water bulges slightly above the rim of the glass. The surface skin, caused by cohesion, keeps the water from spilling over. But the skin stretches only so much before it breaks. You can also see cohesion in a heaping spoonful of water.

SURFACE TENSION

Surface tension is another name for the rubbery skin on the surface of water, that is formed by the cohesion of molecules. An object can rest on water's surface if the object does not have enough weight to break through water's surface tension.

MAGIC FLOATS

CHECKLIST   bowl • water • oil • paper clips • sewing needle

1. Open a paper clip (as shown) to make a holder.
2. Rub oil on a paper clip or needle and rest it on the holder.
3. Gently lower the holder until the clip floats on the water.
4. Carefully remove the holder.

RESULT   Although the paper clip is made of metal, it is too light to break through the surface tension. The oil on the clip also helps it float, since oil is lighter than water. Notice how the water dents slightly under the clip.

FLOATING

An object floats or sinks depending on how much water it pushes aside. When the amount of water **displaced** (pushed aside) weighs more than the object, the object floats. The ability of an object to float is called **buoyancy.**

APPLE BOBBING

CHECKLIST   large tub • water • apples • coins

1. Push coins into apples.
2. Float apples in a tub of water.
3. Players with hands behind their backs try to remove the apples with their teeth. Use stemless apples for older players.

RESULT   The apples are buoyant, thus easy to bite into. An apple is buoyant because it contains air, unlike a rock. When any object weighs less than the water it pushes aside, the object floats.

DISPERSION

Water and food coloring are made up of tiny particles called molecules. When food coloring mixes with water, their molecules blend together. When food coloring's molecules **disperse** (spread out) in water, the color becomes less strong. We call this action **dispersion.**

"HOLES" IN WATER

CHECKLIST   drinking glass • water • food coloring

1. Add several drops of food coloring in a glass of water.
2. Allow the glass to stand undisturbed overnight.

RESULT   Active water molecules push around the less active food coloring molecules. The food coloring molecules quickly move into holes (spaces) between the water molecules. After a time, water and coloring equally **blend** (mix) together.

16

LEACHING

Rainwater **leaches** (removes) harmful chemicals from the soil and air and washes them into rivers and streams. Eventually the waterways deposit these chemicals into drinking-water supplies and oceans, causing **pollution.**

SUN TEA

CHECKLIST   very large glass jar •
water • tea bags • cup

1. Fill a large jar with water.
2. Submerge three or more tea bags into the water. Screw on the lid, holding the strings of the tea bags in place.
3. Set the jar in the sun for six hours.

RESULT   The water leached out tea molecules from the tea leaves. The molecules slowly dispersed in the water. The sun heated the beverage.

17

SOLVENT

Water can act as a **solvent,** which means it is able to dissolve other substances. Water helps molecules in salt crystals to **disperse** (scatter) in the water. Salt molecules then fill in the "holes" between the water molecules.

RAINBOW GARDEN

CHECKLIST   charcoal briquettes • disposable aluminum pan • measuring cup • salt • ammonia • laundry bluing • food coloring • can

1. Squeeze food coloring on briquettes arranged in a pan.
2. In a can, mix ½ cup each of water, bluing, and ammonia. Mix in a ½ cup salt. Pour this liquid over the briquettes.
3. Set the pan in a warm place.
4. Add new solution when needed.

RESULT   The briquettes absorb fluids. When water evaporates on the briquettes, salt recrystallizes around "power bits" in the bluing. Ammonia, a better solvent than water, makes crystals form more rapidly.

SATURATION

Water, a solvent, **dissolves** substances like sugar. Hot water dissolves and holds more sugar than cold water. But water can only dissolve so much. Eventually, water becomes **saturated** (can no longer dissolve sugar) and crystals collect on the bottom of the container.

ROCK CANDY

CHECKLIST   drinking glass • water • drinking straw • cord • washer

1. With an adult's help, stir sugar in a glass of hot water, until the water is saturated.
2. Tie a washer and a straw to a piece of cord.
3. Wet the cord, roll it in sugar, and very gently place it in the water, resting the straw on the rim.
4. After a time, when new crystals form on the cord, reheat the water, dissolve more sugar, and return the cord to the glass.

RESULT   As the water cools, the extra dissolved sugar recrystallizes and is attracted to the sugar clinging to the cord. Crystals attach themselves to other crystals.

19

DENSITY

The main ingredients in ginger ale and strawberry gelatin dessert are water, sugar, flavoring, and coloring. But the gelatin is thicker than the soda pop because it contains an extra ingredient, gelatin. The more ingredients you add to water the **denser** it becomes.

SUBMARINE EGG

CHECKLIST drinking glass • water • salt • spoon • fresh egg

1. Mix salt in a glass half-filled with water until crystals collect on the bottom.
2. Float an egg in the saltwater.
3. Carefully pour fresh water into the glass, along the side.

RESULT Buoyancy, not magic, keeps the egg suspended in the middle of the water. Because saltwater is heavier (denser) than fresh water, it stays at the bottom of the glass. The saltwater's greater density makes the egg buoyant.

20

SOUND

Moving water makes sounds, such as the splashing of a waterfall, the crashing of an ocean wave, and the plop-plopping of a dripping faucet. Standing water usually does not produce sound unless it has the addition of an outside force.

GLASS CHIMES

CHECKLIST 3 or more drinking glasses the same size • water • food coloring • spoon

1. Fill drinking glasses with different levels of water. Add food coloring to each.
2. Hit the glasses with a spoon below the water line to create different sounds.

RESULT When a spoon strikes a glass, it creates **vibrations** that travel through the water. The **echo** from the vibrations produces a ringing sound. The more water in the glass, the further vibrations must travel and the lower the sound.

REFRACTION

When **light waves** pass through water, sometimes the water plays tricks with your eyes. Big bodies of water, like the oceans, sometime look blue. A glass filled to the brim, without a water line, gives the appearance of an empty glass.

BENT BEAM

CHECKLIST   drinking glass • water • unsharpened pencil

1. Put a pencil into a glass of water.
2. Stand the pencil straight or slant it at different angles.

RESULT   A beam of light travels in straight lines and cannot turn or bend. But when light waves enter water, they travel in a different line of direction. Where the pencil enters the water, the light rays send the image of the pencil to your eyes from another direction. We call this **refraction.** That's why the pencil appears broken.

MAGNIFICATION

A magnifying glass helps you see small things bigger. A microscope helps you see things you can't normally see. A telescope brings the stars closer. All three have **magnifying lenses.** A glass of water can also act like a magnifying lens.

MAGNIFYING GLASS

CHECKLIST   drinking glass • water • picture

1. Fill a glass with water.
2. Place a picture against the back of the glass.

RESULT   A magnifying lens is thicker in the middle than at its edges. Like a lens, a glass of water is thicker in the middle than at the sides and it can **magnify** (make larger) a picture behind it.

DISPLACEMENT

Unlike a Ping-Pong ball that is filled with air, a rock is very heavy. The rock is heavy because its molecules are packed closely together, leaving little room for air. When placed in water, the Ping-Pong ball floats while the rock sinks. (See Floating, page 15.)

SINK LIKE A ROCK

CHECKLIST drinking glass • tape or marker • rock

1. On a glass half-filled with water, mark the water line with tape or marker.
2. Place a stone inside the glass.

RESULT Because the rock weighed more than the water it **displaced** (pushed aside) the water and sank. The displaced water moved up into the **air space** in the glass. The mark shows how much water the rock displaced.

TEMPERATURE

We drink water at many temperatures. Warm water, mixed with honey and lemon juice, soothes a sore throat. Ice cubes in water cools us on a hot summer day. Leave a glass of water on a table and the water will become the temperature of the room.

COLD WATER SINKS

CHECKLIST   drinking glass • water • dish • ice cubes

1. Place a glass of water on a dish.
2. Place ice cubes around the bottom half of the glass.
3. After fifteen minutes, feel the water at the top of the glass.

RESULT   The water at the top is not cold. Molecules in cold water are close together, making it **denser** (heavier) than warm water. The heavy cold water stays at the bottom. Had you added a few cubes into the glass from the top, the cooled top water still would have sunk to the bottom, pushing up the warmer water.

SEEPAGE

"Water always finds its path." That's a popular saying. Water is a liquid which flows downward because of gravity. Water, **seeping** (slowly passing) through fissures (cracks) in rocks for millions of years, forms beautiful caves deep inside the earth.

MARBLEIZED EGGS

CHECKLIST   small bowl • water • tea bags • eggs

1. Ask an adult to make you a bowl of tea. For strong color, use several tea bags.
2. Crack, but don't remove, the shells of hard-boiled eggs.
3. Soak the eggs in the tea in the refrigerator for several hours before you peel away the shells.

RESULT   The tea slowly seeped through the cracks in the shells and stained the white of the eggs with tea in a marbleized pattern. At Easter, use food coloring.

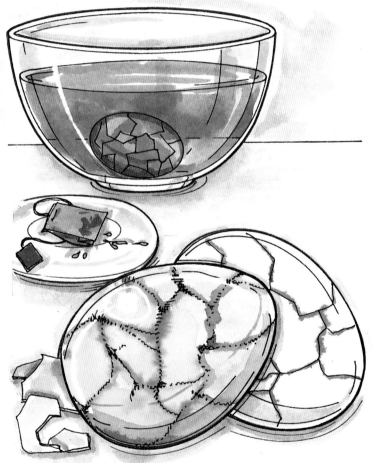

RECONSTITUTION

Fruit remains fresh for only a short time before it begins to rot. Fruit contains water, which is necessary for bacteria to grow. If you remove the water, the fruit can last a long time. Astronauts take dried fruit and food into space.

BLOW-UP FRUIT

CHECKLIST   bowl • warm water • dried fruits • waxed paper

1. Soak dried fruit in warm water.
2. When the fruit reaches its original size, place it on waxed paper, until the surface water dries.

RESULT   Dehydration is the loss of water through **evaporation.** Water molecules evaporate when they enter the air as **vapor** (tiny drops of water). When dehydrated fruit sits in water, it absorbs (soaks up) water, replacing what it lost. Reconstituted fruit does not look exactly as it did when it was fresh.

ROOTS

Most plants have **roots**. Water and important minerals enter the plants through the roots to aid in the plant's growth and life. Roots, especially those of large trees, can grow very deep into the earth searching for water.

WINDOWSILL GARDEN

CHECKLIST   jar or pan • water • onion, beet, turnip, carrot, or parsnip • knife • toothpicks

1. Push toothpicks into an onion, around its middle. Rest the toothpicks on the rim of a jar that has enough water to cover the onion's bottom.
2. Cut away 1½ inches (3.75 cm) of the top of root vegetables. Cut away any leaves. Sit the tops in shallow water.

RESULT   After a time, the onion and root tops begin to grow roots. Because the tops (and onion) store food and the tops still have the base of the plant's stem at its center, they can start new plants.

28

GERMINATION

All living things need water to grow. Although dried beans are no longer fresh, they contain all the "information" to grow into a plant. Water helps start the growing process. Before leaves form, beans use their own supplies of food to grow roots.

BEAN SPROUTS

CHECKLIST   jar with lid • paper towels • water • dried beans

1. Place wet paper towels in a jar.
2. Place dried beans in the jar, against the glass. The radicle (indent) faces up.
3. Turn the jar upside down when roots and greenery form.

RESULT   When leaves grow, beans use light to make food. Green shoots grow upward toward the light (**heliotropism**); roots grow downward toward gravity (**geotropism**). When you turn the jar upside down, the roots and shoots change direction. Again the shoots grow up toward the light and the roots toward gravity. Plants also seek water (**hydrotropism**).

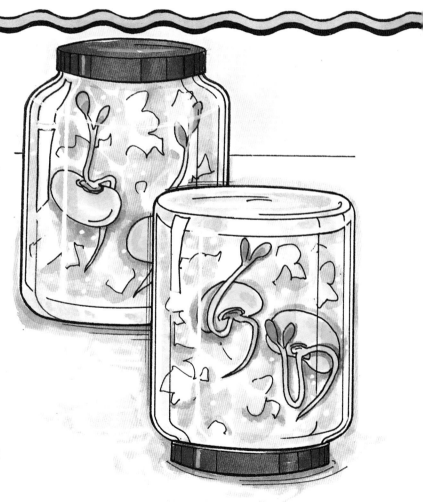

29

HABITAT

A **habitat** is a place where an animal or a plant lives. A bat's habitat is a cave and a monkey's is a tree. Pets, like cats and dogs, share people's habitats. Fish, because they do not breathe air, must have their own watery habitats. How does a fish breath? Water flows into a fish's mouth with oxygen dissolved in it. The fish's gills take in the oxygen and give out carbon dioxide. Water flows out through the gill openings.

PAINTED FISHBOWL

CHECKLIST fishbowl • fish • brush • poster paints

With poster paints, paint a fun scene on the back of an existing, or a new, fishbowl.

RESULT The **depth** (amount) of the water and the refraction of light (see Refraction, page 22) makes the colors of the paint seem lighter. The water also magnifies the picture (see Magnification, page 23).

WATER IS A
LIQUID IN MOTION

THE JOURNEY OF WATER

Wind, gravity, and the moon are natural forces that keep water on the move. Machines, like windmills, turbine engines, and water pumps in automobiles, also move water. Pressure from giant water tanks forces water through the pipes in our homes.

Water from melting snow trickles into small creeks (brooks) where frogs and other animals live. The creeks empty into rivers and lakes and larger waterways where fishermen can hook a bass.

Rivers twist, turn, and fall over rocks as waterfalls. Eventually great rivers empty into the even greater oceans.

THE CYCLE OF WATER

The **cycle** of water is the story of movement. Water falls from clouds as a **liquid** in the form of raindrops and as **crystals** in the form of snowflakes. As a **solid,** it floats on rivers and oceans as ice floes and icebergs. Eventually, it returns to the clouds as **vapor** (gas), and the cycle is repeated.

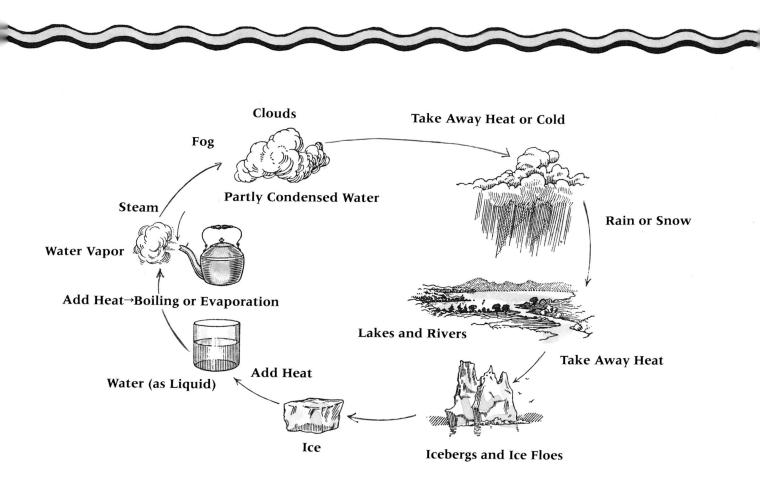

THE CYCLE OF WATER

GRAVITY

When water is contained, its surface is **level** (flat). That means that no part is higher than the other. It also means that the surface is parallel with the **horizon.** We can see water's level surface by looking out over a large lake or an ocean. **Gravity,** which pulls liquids toward the earth, makes them level.

LEVEL

CHECKLIST   jar with lid • water

1. Fill a jar half-full with water. Screw on the lid.
2. Slowly turn the jar on an angle, on its side, upside down, and back to its original position.

RESULT   Although water moves to fill in the empty space in a turning jar, the surface remains level because of gravity's equal downward pull.

AGITATION

Overturn in a lake starts when heavier surface water, cooled by the air temperature, sinks. When it hits the bottom, it **agitates** the **sediment** (heavy particles) in the warmer water. The sediment rises, making the water muddy.

SNOW GLOBE

CHECKLIST jar with lid • water • sparkles • plastic flowers • plastic toys • glue gun

1. Ask an adult to glue plastic flowers and toys on the inside of a jar lid with a glue gun. You can also use any glue that is not water-soluble.
2. Add sparkles to the jar. Fill the jar to the top with water and screw on the lid. Shake.

RESULT Shaking the jar agitates the water inside. Water currents, created by agitation, pick up the glitter at the bottom of the jar and scatter it.

35

VORTEX

The planet Jupiter has a giant red spot that scientists believe is a **vortex,** a giant swirling hurricane made of dust and gases. On earth, a whirling vortex of air is a **whirlwind.** A water vortex is a **whirlpool.**

GLITTERING WHIRLPOOL

CHECKLIST   jar • water • glitter • drinking straw

1. Add glitter to a jar three-quarters-full with water.
2. Stir the water quickly in a circular motion with a straw.

RESULT   Stirring water in a swirling motion agitates it. The agitation creates a center **depression** (hole). The swirling water picks up the glitter and pulls it toward the depression, the same way a tornado, a funnel of swirling air, sucks in everything in its way.

SOLUTION

In cooking, to **blend** means to mix different ingredients together thoroughly. Blending creates new mixtures. If you blend blue and yellow paints together, you get green paint. Red food coloring in clear water creates a pink liquid. And when another liquid or solid **dissolves** in water, we call this liquid a **solution.**

TART & SWEET

CHECKLIST glass or mug • water • spoon • lemon • sugar

1. Fill a glass or mug with water.
2. Stir sugar and lemon juice into the water until it tastes good.

RESULT When sugar dissolves in water, sugar molecules evenly fill in spaces between the water molecules. When you add lemon juice, the lemon molecules evenly fill in spaces between the sugar and water molecules. Your tongue blends the sweet and sour tastes. When thoroughly blended this mixture is called a **solution.** If lemon pulp also floats in it, it is called a **suspension.**

EMULSION

Plain water floats on saltwater because it is lighter. Warm water floats on cold water because it is lighter. Oil floats on water because, it too, is lighter. And no matter how hard you shake oil and vinegar in a bottle, the oil always rises to the top. This combination of liquids that do not blend is called an **emulsion.**

SEPARATION

CHECKLIST   jar with lid • water • cooking oil

1. Add some water to a jar. Add an equal amount of oil. Tightly close the jar.
2. Shake the jar vigorously.

RESULT   The oil breaks up into **droplets** because oil molecules are different than water molecules, and they cannot blend together. A water molecule has two **atoms** of hydrogen and one of oxygen (H_2O). An oil molecule has hundreds of atoms, and it contains carbon as well as hydrogen and oxygen.

PRESSURE

Pressure is force pushing against a surface. A **barometer** is an instrument that measures the pressure in the air (**atmospheric pressure**). It is used to forecast changes in the weather. Water, as well as air, exerts pressure.

AGAINST GRAVITY

CHECKLIST   glass • water • cardboard or poster board

1. Fill a glass with water.
2. Cut a cardboard square larger than the rim of the glass.
3. Press the cardboard on the rim and carefully turn the glass upside down over the sink. Remove your hand.

RESULT   The cardboard stays in place. The **air pressure** outside the glass is greater than the pressure of the water. Because the outside air is stonger, it pushes against the cardboard, keeping the water from pouring out. The air pressure is greater than the **water pressure.**

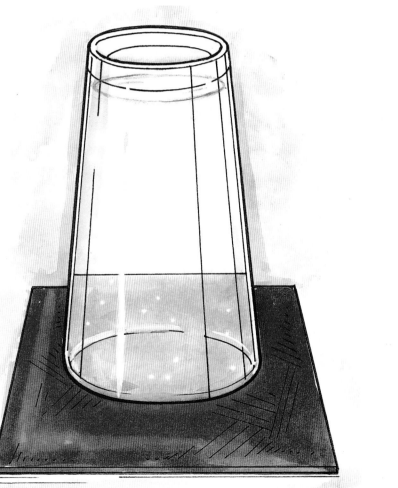

HEAT

Have you noticed that the water in the ocean or in a swimming pool is warmer at your waist than at your feet? The sun, or even warm air, heats the water near the surface. Because warm water is lighter than cool water, it remains at the top.

UNDERWATER ERUPTION

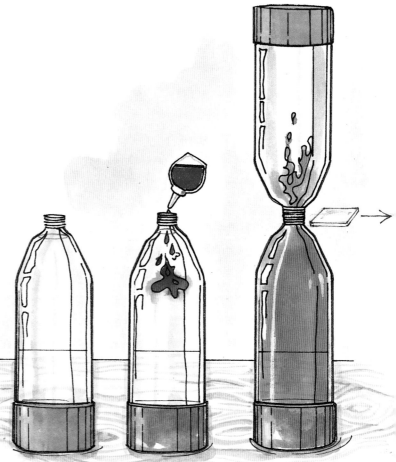

CHECKLIST 2 soda pop bottles • water • food coloring • paper

1. In a sink or outdoors, add food coloring to a bottle filled with very warm water. Shake.
2. Hold a paper square over the mouth of a bottle filled with cold water. Turn the bottle upside down.
3. Carefully rest the bottle's neck on the neck of the warm water bottle. Holding the necks tightly, pull the paper away.

RESULT The colored warm water rises into the cold water when the two meet. Molecules pull away from each other in warm water, making it lighter than cold water.

CURRENTS

Currents are streams of water flowing through large bodies of water. In the seas, there are deep, surface, and drift currents, which can be either warm or cold. Fish and other marine life ride the currents to feed and to migrate.

GAME IN A JAR

CHECKLIST jars with lids • water • food coloring • small glass • pennies • dice • rubber washers • drinking straw

1. Stand a small glass in a large jar filled with colored water. Stir, then drop pennies into the glass (A).
2. Pass a piece of straw through washers floating in a jar of colored water (B).
3. Shake dice in a jar filled with colored water (C).

RESULT Moving water creates currents. Currents make it hard for pennies to drop in straight lines (A) and for a straw to pass through washers (B). Currents make it easy for dice to flip and turn (C).

41

ABSORPTION

If soil did not **absorb** (soak up) water, water would never reach a plant's roots. Some things absorb water better than others, like flour and paper. Other things do not absorb water, like stones and gold. Try this magic trick to amaze your friends.

DISAPPEAR LIKE MAGIC

CHECKLIST   clear glass • paper cup • water • sponge

1. Add a few spoonfuls of water to a clear glass.
2. Fold a dry sponge. Push it to the bottom of a paper cup.
3. Slowly pour the water into the paper cup. Don't let anyone see the sponge.
4. After a few seconds, turn the paper cup upside down. Like magic, the water seems to have disappeared.

RESULT   A dry sponge has lots of **air pockets** to absorb and hold water. Things that are dry absorb more water than those that are wet.

BUOYANCY

A cargo ship is heavy, but it does not sink. When empty, the ship sits high in the water and much of its hull (the main body) is above the water line. When filled with heavy cargo, the ship sinks deeper into othe water but still remains **buoyant** (able to float).

SAILBOAT RACE

CHECKLIST   walnut shells • play clay • toothpicks • paper • crayon • tape

1. Press small clay balls into the centers of half-shells of walnuts.
2. Tape small paper sails, each with a number, to toothpicks.
3. Push the toothpicks into the clay balls.
4. Place the boats in water. Players blow on the sails.

RESULT   Because a shell is filled with air, it **displaces** (pushes aside) enough water to keep it afloat, even with the weight of a ball of clay inside. (See Floating, page 15.)

RIPPLES & REFLECTIONS

Ripples are tiny **seismic** (caused by force) **waves** of energy moving on the surface of water. Wind is one force that creates enough energy to make water ripple. Objects dropped into water create another force. Ripples break up **reflections** on water.

ROCK SKIPPING

CHECKLIST   small flat rocks • large body of water

1. Throw a rock at water with force. The angle of the throw should be as parallel and as close to the water's surface as possible.
2. Notice how reflections break up on the level surface of the water when it is disturbed.

RESULT   When a rock hits water, it sinks, leaving an empty space on the surface. The water the rock pushed aside forms a ring that **expands** (grows larger) as it moves outward. The ring, along with **vibrations** caused by the rock hitting the water, creates more expanding rings.

44

DRIPPING

Dripping water does not flow but falls. Leaky faucets drip. Raindrops on leaves drip to the ground, pulled by gravity. Rainwater seeps into the ground, dissolving minerals from soil and rocks.

Sometimes it seeps into deep underground caves. Over millions of years this creates icicle-shaped mineral formations called **stalagmites** and **stalactites**.

WATER CLOCK

CHECKLIST paper plates • paper • large jar or pot • water • needle • paper fasteners • nails • hammer

1. With a needle, make a tiny pinhole in the middle of the bottom of two or more cups.
2. Attach the cups to paper plates with paper fasteners. (See picture.)
3. Nail the plates to a tree or tape then to a wall, one above the other. Stand a jar under the bottom cup.
4. Fill the top cup with water.

RESULT The pressure (force) of the water and the air above it forces water through the holes. The clock runs during the time the water drips into the cups and empties into the jar. A **water clock** is an instrument designed to measure time by the fall or flow of a quantity of water.

RAINDROPS

When water vapor rises to the colder atmosphere above, water molecules stick together to form **droplets.** The droplets attach to dust particles, which we see as **clouds.** When many droplets collect together in the clouds, they become too heavy to stay up and fall as rain.

DROPLET PAINTING

CHECKLIST   paper • watercolor or tempera paints • paintbrush • rain

1. Paint a picture or a color design on paper.
2. Set the paper outside in a light rain. For a little spatter, keep the paper out for a few seconds. The longer the paper stays out, the more the picture will blur.

RESULT   Watercolor and tempera paints are **water-soluble;** that means they dissolve in water. When a raindrop hits the paper, the liquid dissolves some of the paint. Water and paint **spatters** (splashes or scatters) outward because of the impact.

46

FLUIDITY

Water **flows** because it is a **liquid,** and gravity pulls liquids downward. We think of flowing water as wide as a mighty river or as narrow as a winding creek (brook). But water has the amazing ability to flow in a line as thin as a hair. We call this **fluidity.**

QUILL PEN

CHECKLIST   large feather • utility knife • food coloring • glass • paper

1. Find or buy a feather.
2. Ask an adult to help you cut the tip of the feather's quill into a pen point, using a utility knife. Trim away part of the tip to create a point. Cut a short slit into the middle of the point.
3. Dip the point in food coloring and draw pictures and write words.

RESULT   The slit holds a tiny supply of **fluid.** When writing, the slit spreads apart slightly, releasing the coloring.

STREAM

When water flows at a steady speed, we say it **streams.** The speed that water flows in a creek depends on the amount of water feeding into it from rain or snow. Pressure forces water to stream out of a faucet, from a slow trickle to a fast flow. People use this movement to transport themselves and goods.

WATER SLIDE

CHECKLIST long strip of thick plastic sheeting • garden hose

1. Lay plastic sheeting on grass. A sloping ground is best.
2. Set the garden hose so that a small flow of water streams down the sheeting.
3. Slide and belly flop down the water slide.

RESULT A layer of water creates a slippery cushion between you and the plastic. The cushion of water eliminates friction, which would prevent you from sliding.

DIVERSION

When you change the flow of water, you **divert** it. In nature, flowing water sometimes changes course because of **erosion,** which is the wearing away of the land. Sometimes people purposely divert rivers to direct fresh water to places where it is needed. Farmers sometimes use pipes and artificial canals to **irrigate** land.

WATER PIPES

CHECKLIST   paper-towel tubes • bathroom-tissue tubes • scissors • heavy tape • pitcher • water

1. Cut across the length of bathroom-tissue tubes. From this cut, cut out an oval shape in the middle.
2. Fold the cut tubes to form elbows (right angles). Tape in place.
3. Cut some paper-towel tubes in half.
4. Create a pipe system by inserting the half tubes and whole tubes into both elbows and uncut tubes.

RESULT   You can change the direction that water flows by guiding it through pipes. They act as **conduits.** A river naturally twists and turns. This natural **meander pattern** (winding) of a river can also be seen on a window or windshield when rainwater flows down.

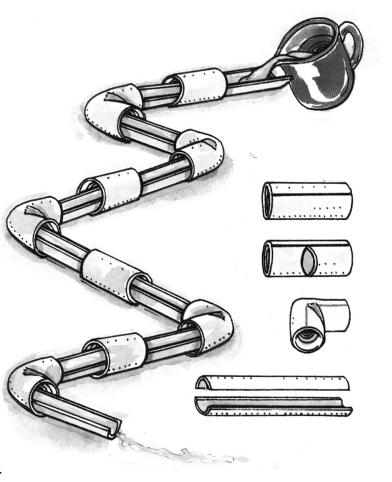

SIPHONING

When you first sip soda pop through a straw, you remove the air. **Suction** is the force that pulls the soda into the space the air occupied in the straw. **Siphoning,** the transferring of fluid from one glass to another, begins with suction. The tube used for taking liquid out of a container and passing it to a lower level is called a **siphon.**

LEAP FROG

CHECKLIST 2 glasses the same size • apple juice • flexible plastic tubing or rubber hose

1. Place a glass of apple juice higher than an empty glass.
2. Place one end of a tube in the juice. Suck through the other end, pulling juice to your mouth. Quickly place your finger over the end you sucked to keep the juice from flowing backwards.
3. Place the end of the tube into the empty glass. Remove your finger.

WEIGHT

Why does water leave a faucet with the turn of a handle? What would fire-fighters do if the water in their hoses could not reach second-floor windows? In both cases, **water pressure,** which exerts a great force, sends water shooting outward.

WATER SPOUTS

CHECKLIST   milk carton • paper or foam cups • nail • water

1. With a nail, make three equally spaced holes in the side of a carton (A).
2. Make several holes in the bottom of a cup (B).
3. Make several holes close together in the bottom of a second cup (C).
4. Fill each with water.

RESULT   Water has **weight,** which creates pressure. **(A)** The lowest hole has the most water above it, which creates the most forceful stream. **(B)** Gravity creates equal spouts. **(C)** If you pinch the spouts together, they join because water molecules are **attracted** to each other. (See Cohesion, page 13.)

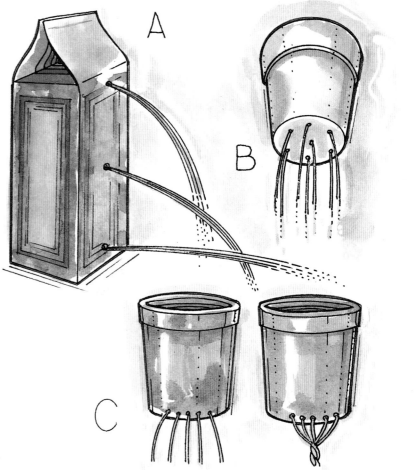

51

ENERGY

People have invented ways to use the power of air and water to make their work easier. The **vanes** (blades) of a windmill catch the power of wind, and change it to mechanical **energy.** In the same way, waterwheels use the power of water. A simple waterwheel creates energy that can be used to power a small motor. A paddlewheel boat uses a large waterwheel to move the boat.

WATERWHEEL

CHECKLIST 2 plastic plates • glue • scissors • poster board • water • pencil

1. Glue the bottoms of two plates together. Dry.
2. Make a hole in the center of the plates with a sharp pencil.
3. Cut matching slits into the sides of both plates.
4. Push cardboard rectangles of the same size into each two, creating blades.
5. Insert the pencil into the hole, hold the ends, and place the wheel under running water.

RESULT The force of the water on a blade moves the wheel enough for another blade to move into its place. The wheel spins blade by blade.

SPREADING

Water in a bucket, when emptied on the ground, does not stay together as it did in the bucket. It **spreads** out. This happens because water is a liquid, a substance that flows. Gravity, pulling the water equally, makes the water surface spread out evenly.

WATER BLOTS

CHECKLIST   paper • water • food coloring

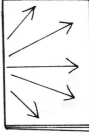

1. Drop food coloring onto half a sheet of paper.
2. Fold the paper in half. Press down on the paper in all directions with your hand, starting at the crease and moving to the edges.

RESULT   Food coloring is water with dye (color) mixed in. Folding the paper forces the blots of color to spread into each other. Some food coloring molecules mix with others, forming new colors.

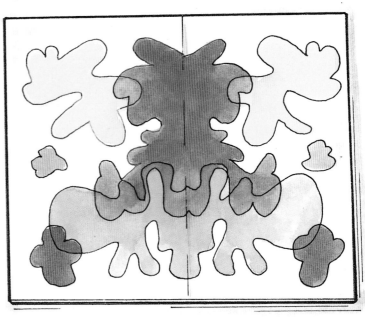

BLEEDING

You must mix oil and tempera paints together to get different colors because they contain little or no water. Because you mix watercolor paint with a lot of water, different colors form when one watery color **bleeds** (mixes) into another color.

TEE-SHIRT

CHECKLIST   tee-shirt • fabric dyes • paintbrush • bowls • water • waxed paper

1. Mix fabric dyes in bowls.
2. Wet a tee-shirt and ring out most of the water.
3. Put sheets of waxed paper inside the shirt.
4. Dab colors onto the shirt with a paintbrush. Remove the paper when the shirt is dry.

RESULT   Color molecules in fabric dyes move freely between the water molecules on the wet shirt, as well as mixing with each other. They bleed (escape or flow) into each other.

CAPILLARITY

Have you ever heard of a waterfall that flows *up* instead of falling down? Or a river that flows upstream? Water flows downward because of gravity. Gravity is a force inside the earth that draws all objects toward the center of the planet.

But in a plant, **capillarity** can change the direction water usually flows.

TINTED CELERY

CHECKLIST   2 small glasses • food coloring • water • stalk of celery with a lot of leaves

1. Cut away the bottom half of a celery stalk. Cut a slit into the stalk, up to the nub where the leaves begin.
2. Insert the stalk halves into glasses of water. Each glass has a strong concentrate of food coloring in a different color.

RESULT   Water flows upward *against* gravity in a plant. In stems and stalks, there are countless hairline fibers. Water molecules, pulling together, grow strong enough to move upward, using the fibers as a ladder. (See Cohesion, page 13.) This is called **capillary action.** The water feeds the plant with nutrients from the soil.

REJUVENATION

The earth is unique in the Milky Way solar system because it has large bodies of water. All living plants and animals need water to live. If a plant (or person) does not drink, it withers. If a withered plant drinks, it **rejuvenates** (perks up).

THIRSTY PLANTS

CHECKLIST   potted plant • water

1. Stop watering a potted plant until it droops.
2. Water the plant and watch it perk up. Ask an adult to take time-lapse shots of the plant's rejuvenation with a standard camera or video camera.

RESULT   **Evaporation** is the loss of water molecules into the air. The warmer the air, the faster a plant loses water from its leaves. A plant's cells slowly lose their storehouse of water through evaporation and they shrink. Water, absorbed by a thirsty plant, replaces lost water and plumps up cells. The plant regains its original vigor and appears young again. We call this **rejuvenation.**

WATER IS A SOLID, CRYSTAL & VAPOR

WATER'S OTHER PERSONALITIES

Water is not just a liquid. It is also a solid, crystal, and vapor. You see its other forms on cloudy days, in cold winters, or when you peek into a refrigerator.

We've been told that Jack Frost is an elf who visits houses on winter nights to paint windows with beautiful, frosty **crystals.**

Although clouds look like they're solid, they are actually made up of water vapor, which is a **gas.** It's fun to see pictures in clouds.

At the North Pole, there is no land, just a vast wilderness of ice and snow. Under the thick layers of ice and snow of the South Pole there is land.

FREEZING

Molecules **expand** both when water boils and when it **freezes.** As water cools to 39.2° F (4° C), its molecules grow close together, making it *heavier.* This is its greatest **density.** Molecules in water nearing the freezing point, pull away from each other (expand), making ice *lighter* and less dense.

GROWING WATER

CHECKLIST   jar • water • crayon or china marker

1. Fill a jar three-fourths-full with water.
2. Mark the water line on the jar with a crayon.
3. Place the jar in a freezer until the water freezes.

RESULT   As water freezes, molecules expand. In a container, ice that is forming moves into the air space, rising above the original water line. In a jar filled with water and the lid screwed on, expanding molecules have no air space to move into. Ice expands against the jar, breaking it.

SLIDING

When the top layer of water freezes in a pond or lake, it forms a protective "cover." This ice cover keeps the water and the fish below from freezing. When the ice cover is thick enough, we can enjoy the pond or lake for slippery fun.

SUMMER HOCKEY

CHECKLIST   plastic sheeting • 2 milk cartons • corrugated cardboard • 2 pencils or wooden dowels • ice cube

1. Cut away the bottom half of two milk containers. Cut away one side of each for the goals.
2. Lay plastic sheeting on the ground. Stand a goal at each end, open side facing in.
3. Hockey sticks are pencils or dowels pushed into cardboard rectangles. An ice cube is the puck.

RESULT   Cubes move without friction on plastic because they glide on a layer of water, resulting from the melting ice.

FRACTURES

Icebergs are large, floating **masses** (chunks) of frozen water that break away (**fracture**) from ice formed on land and in seas. Some are as large as buildings. Most of an iceberg is under water. The saying, "It's only the tip of the iceberg," means there is something more than what you can see. **Ice floes** are large, flat pieces of ice that float on rivers and seas.

SNOW CONE

CHECKLIST   ice cubes • clean dish cloth • hammer • fruit syrup • paper cup • straw

1. Wrap ice cubes in a dish cloth.
2. Hit the cloth with a hammer, crushing the cubes inside into tiny chips. (Ask an adult for help.)
3. Fill a cup with chips. Pour syrup over them. Add a straw.

RESULT   Frozen water is **brittle,** which means it's not **flexible** (does not bend). Its brittleness, a result of its cold temperature, helps ice to break under the force of an impact.

FORMATION

Ice carvers cut and shape ice into swans and fish and other forms. Nature also shapes ice into works of art. If weather conditions are right, icicles form in all sizes, from tiny frozen drops on bushes to huge spears hanging from roofs. We enjoy these natural **formations** as well as the artist's creations.

ICICLES

CHECKLIST   2 tall cans • twig • cord • pitcher • water

1. On a day below freezing, lay a twig across two cans outside. Tie one or two strings to the twig.
2. Pour a little cold water onto the strings every few minutes.

RESULT   Naturally forming **icicles** occur when snow, melting in the sun, hits a cold surface, like under the edge of a roof. The cold draws away the water's heat. Drop by drop, the water freezes on itself. Icicles are fragile and shatter when they drop.

HEAT ENERGY

With water, expect the unexpected. A tray of ice cubes in a tub of warm water melts away faster than those in a bowl of hot water. Why? The water in the bowl is hotter, but the total **heat energy** in the tub of warm water is greater.

FREEZING RATE

CHECKLIST   2 glasses • water • food coloring

1. Fill a glass with cold water. Fill another glass with hot water (Ask an adult for help.) Add food coloring to each.
2. Place the glasses in the freezer.
3. Check every so often.

RESULT   In temperatures below freezing, both hot and cold water lose heat. But hot water **evaporates** much faster than cold water, thus it loses a great amount of heat energy. Therefore, hot water freezes faster than cold because its temperature drops faster.

REFRIGERATION

Refrigeration involves keeping a cool temperature in an enclosed area. A refrigerator keeps food fresh for a long time. Refrigerated box cars on trains allow produce and frozen foods to travel great distances without spoiling.

ICE CREAM

CHECKLIST   pot • clean tin can • ice • coarse salt • half-and-half • vanilla • sugar • spoon

1. Place a can inside a pot.
2. Place a layer of ice cubes or ice chips in the pot around the can. Sprinkle a lot of salt on the ice. Add layers of ice and salt up to the top of the can.
3. Fill the can half full with half-and-half. Add vanilla and a little sugar. Stir for a long time.

RESULT   Salt melts ice. It also makes the ice colder. Stirring pushes the milk against the can, and "heat" in the milk is transferred to the ice. The mixture becomes so cold, it freezes into a soft ice cream.

FROST

Frost occurs overnight when water vapor (tiny water particles) rises into the air from the warm ground. The vapor condenses (packs together) forming **dewdrops.** As the temperature falls, the dewdrops freeze into **ice crystals** called frost.

JACK FROST

CHECKLIST   china plate • petroleum jelly or cooking oil

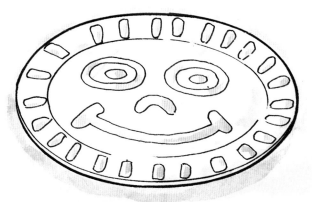

1. Using your finger, draw a design on a clean plate with petroleum jelly.
2. Place the plate in the freezer next to a plastic bowl of hot water. (Ask an adult for help.)
3. After a time, remove the plate.

RESULT   A china plate absorbs cold more than petroleum jelly. In a freezer, water vapor rises from hot water. The vapor **condenses** and freezes into crystals that attach to the dish, that is colder than the petroleum jelly.

ICE CRYSTALS

A **salt crystal** is a six-sided cube, although a perfect cube is hard to find. Salt crystals form lopsided because they grow crowded on top of each other. **Ice crystals** are also six-sided, but they are almost perfect because they fall separately. We call these falling ice crystals "snowflakes."

SNOWFLAKE CATCHER

CHECKLIST black or dark colored felt • heavy cardboard • glue • magnifying glass • snowflakes

1. Glue black felt on a piece of cardboard.
2. Catch several snowflakes on the felt.
3. Study the ice crystals under a magnifying glass.

RESULT When ice crystals fall on your skin, they absorb heat and melt. When they fall on felt, they rest on tiny fibers standing above the surface. Cold air, circulating under the snowflakes, keeps them in a frozen state long enough for you to study them.

ADHESION

Snow that is as fine as powder or heavy with water does not have fully developed six-sided crystals. But fully developed **snowflakes** are able to **adhere** (stick) to a surface as narrow as a telephone wire and pile high on itself. They are nearly perfect, six-sided ice crystals.

ROLLED SNOW ANIMALS

CHECKLIST   snow • colored paper or poster board • scissors • odds and ends (for faces)

1. Roll snow that is not too wet or powdery into balls of all sizes.
2. Create animals using snowballs of different sizes.
3. Make faces with paper cutouts, drinking straws, and odds and ends, like bottle caps and prunes.

RESULT   Snowflakes have the ability to collect high on surfaces or to adhere to each other when rolled into balls because their jagged pointy sides hook onto each other.

MOLDING & COMPACTING

Glaciers are rivers of ice found in the earth's coldest regions and high mountains. Glaciers form when snowfalls do not melt from year to year and turn into crystals called **firm.** This type of snow is pressed down (**compressed**) under the weight of new snows above it. Because glaciers are made of **compacted** snow, rocks, and soil, the ice is not clear.

BUILDING BLOCKS

CHECKLIST   shoe box or small carton • snow • paper • pole • glue

1. Pack snow into a box or carton and turn it upside down. Lift the box, leaving behind a snow brick.
2. The first rows of bricks form the snow fort's foundation. Stagger rows of bricks on the foundation, for strong walls.
3. Glue a paper flag to a pole and stand it in your fort.

RESULT   A snow drift is not solid but has air surrounding each flake. When you pack snow in a box, the air pushes out and the crystals become compact (press together). This is why you can **mold** them into desired shapes. **Igloos** are made from molded and compacted snow and ice.

VOLUME

Volume is the amount of space inside something, like a glass. "Is a glass half-empty or half-full?" is a question asked about a glass of water. It is neither. The volume of the glass is completely full. Water fills half the glass, air the other half.

An instrument used to measure **precipitation** (falling rain, snow, sleet, mist, or hail) is usually called a **rain gauge.** A **snow stick** is also often used to measure the depth of freshly fallen snow.

PRECIPITATION GAUGE

CHECKLIST   pot • snow • ruler • crayon

1. Set a pot outside in a snow storm.
2. After the snow has stopped, bring the pot into the house.
3. Measure the snow line on the pot and mark it with a crayon. Let the snow melt and mark the water line. Measure it.

RESULT   Air takes up space, so when you measure snow, you also measure the air between the snowflakes. When snow melts into a liquid, the air pushes out. The volume of liquid water measures less than the volume of crystallized water.

CONDENSATION

Water vapor is water in the air in the form of a gas. The more moisture in the air, the more **humid** it is. **Condensation** outdoors occurs when air cools during the night, changing vapor into **dew** (water droplets). Dew collects on grass and cold surfaces.

ICED BEVERAGE

CHECKLIST   drinking glass • beverage • ice cubes

1. Add ice cubes to a glass of a soft drink, juice, water, or any beverage.
2. Let the glass stand for a while. The more humid the air the better.

RESULT   Water vapor surrounds a glass of an iced beverage. When the water vapor touches a cold surface, it cools and condenses into water. The water collects as droplets. When a droplet gets too heavy with water, it rolls down the surface, taking other droplets with it.

TRANSPIRATION

A **hothouse** is a glass building where plants grow. The sun passing through the glass warms the air. **Transpiration** occurs in warm air when the leaves of plants release water molecules through evaporation. The molecules turn into water vapor.

RECYCLING

CHECKLIST   fishbowl or large jar • pebbles • potting soil • small plants • water • plastic wrap

1. Add a layer of pebbles on the bottom of a fishbowl. Add a layer of potting soil.
2. Plant small plants in the soil.
3. Moisten the soil with water.
4. Cover the bowl's opening with plastic wrap. Place the bowl in a sunny spot.

RESULT   Vapor from transpiration touches the cool bowl and collects as droplets that roll down to the soil. Plants drink in the water and transpiration begins again. Plastic prevents vapor from escaping into the air. This recycling makes a **terrarium** a complete system that does not need outside attention.

SUCTION

Suction is the removal of air out of a space, creating a **vacuum.** A vacuum is a space with nothing in it. A plunger uses suction to remove air from a drain pipe in a clogged sink. The vacuum created sucks up the clog, allowing water to drain again.

SUSPENDED SPOON

CHECKLIST   metal teaspoon • breath • nose

1. Exhale on the inside of a spoon.
2. With your head tilted back slightly, press the spoon against your nose.

RESULT   Your breath contains water vapor, which condenses into **mist** (tiny water droplets) when it touches the spoon. The force of the spoon pressed against a nose pushes away both air and mist. A vacuum is created. The spoon stays in place because the water of the mist forms a seal between the spoon and skin, which keeps air from reentering the vacuum.

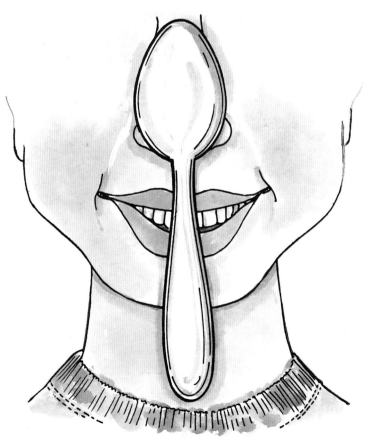

74

MIST

Mist is tiny water droplets suspended in air. Mist, high in the atmosphere and mixed with dust particles, takes the form of **clouds.** Mist that hugs the ground is **fog.** On a winter day, you can see the mist in your breath when you speak.

On rainy days when the sun shines, you sometimes see a **rainbow.** A rainbow displays a **color spectrum,** which contains red, orange, yellow, green, blue, and purple.

RAINBOW

CHECKLIST garden hose • water

1. Facing the sun, turn on a garden hose to create a fine spray. Have a friend stand with his or her back to the sun so that he or she can see the rainbow you create.
2. Spray at a 45° angle with the sun. Keep experimenting until the mist creates colors.

RESULT Water spray contains mist made up of countless tiny water droplets. In sunlight, each droplet acts like a **prism.** A prism, usually made of glass, has angled sides that bend color in sunlight. A **rainbow** forms because the droplets of mist together act like a single prism.

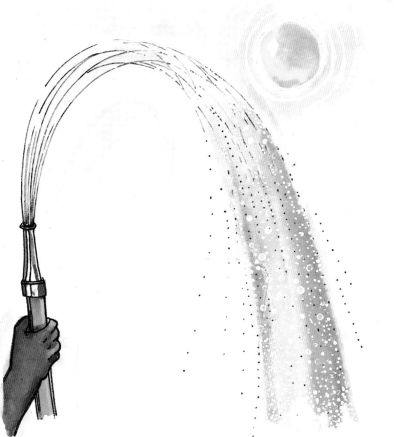

75

STEAM

When water in a teapot boils, the cloud that rises above the spout is not steam. It is actually water that condenses into droplets in the cooler air above the teapot. **Steam,** an invisible gas, is just at the end of the teapot's spout.

HAUNTED HOUSE

CHECKLIST sheet of construction paper • crayons or markers • mug • water • flashlight

1. Fold the sides of a sheet of paper over so that the paper stands.
2. Draw a haunted house on the paper.
3. Ask an adult to make you a mug of very hot water and to place the mug behind the standing house.
4. Turn off the lights. Aim a flashlight beam at the house.

RESULT Steam is visible in the dark when light **reflects** off the surface of tiny water drops in mist, rising from hot water.

FRAGRANCE

We **smell** a fragrance when the molecules of something **aromatic** (having a smell), enters the air and clings to water molecules in the air. Fragrances best reach our noses when they cling to mist, like spray air fresheners and perfumes.

SIMMERING POTPOURRI

CHECKLIST 2 disposable aluminum pie tins • dish • simmering candle • water • flower potpourri

1. Cut out a large hole in the bottom of a pie tin. Cut out openings along the side.
2. Place the cut plate over a candle on a dish. Rest a second pie tin on top of the first.
3. Ask an adult to boil the water and light the candle. Add potpourri and boiling water to the top tin.

RESULT Heated water leaches flower molecules from dried flowers. (See Leaching, page 17.) The mist, rising from the heated water, carries both water and flower molecules, which we **inhale** (breathe in).

77

EVAPORATION

If you leave a glass of water standing overnight in the air, some water **evaporates** (changes into a vapor). Great amounts of water evaporate every day into the **atmosphere** (air) from the oceans. The sun, heating the water's surface, speeds up evaporation.

CROUTONS

CHECKLIST   white bread • waxed paper • grater • plastic knife

1. To make bread crumbs, lay slices of bread on waxed paper. When dry, grate the bread on a grater to form bread crumbs.
2. To make croutons, slice the bread into cubes before drying. Use croutons in soup or salad.

RESULT   Water molecules are in constant motion. Water molecules in bread leap out into the air as water vapor, a gas. When all water molecules evaporate, the solid substances remain.

WATER SMARTS

Here are some water safety tips that make good sense.

SWIMMING

1. Know how to swim before you go into water above your knees.
2. If you eat a big meal, wait 20 minutes before you go into the water.
3. Never dive into water when you are not sure how deep the bottom is.
4. Swim only in areas that have a lifeguard.
5. Do not wade or swim out too far when the waves are rough.
6. If you get caught in an undertow that pulls you into deeper water, do not swim straight toward the beach. Instead, swim at an angle with the beach until you are free of the undertow.
7. If someone is in trouble, throw out anything near you. Chances are something will float.
8. Ask an adult to teach you water safety.

BOATING

1. Always wear a life jacket on a boat.
2. Never stand up in a rowboat. If you must change seats, move in a crouched position along the center of the boat.
3. Learn proper canoeing techniques.
4. Learn how to use rowboat oars properly.

ICE & SNOW

1. Do not walk on frozen water (ponds or lakes) unless signs are posted that tell you it is safe.
2. To prevent broken bones and head injuries, always walk carefully on icy surfaces. Shoes or boots with treads or rubber soles help. Sand helps you walk without slipping. Salt melts ice.
3. Do not stand under icicles, especially if they are melting.
4. Never lick a frozen surface. Your lips and tongue will freeze to it.
5. Do not wander too deeply into snowy woods.
6. Do not ride your bicycle and be careful crossing streets in snowy weather. Remember that cars and trucks cannot stop quickly.

OTHER TIPS

1. Never stand under a tree during an electrical rainstorm.
2. If you get an acidic or salty substance in your eyes, rinse your eyes with plenty of water.
3. Immediately add cold water to a steam or a first-degree burn for 5 minutes.
4. Thoroughly put out a campfire with a soaking water bath.
5. If a pot on the stove catches fire, immediately get an adult or call the fire department. Water may not always be best for putting out a pot fire. Putting a cover or plate over the pot to remove the oxygen is safer.

INDEX

absorption, 42
adherence, 69
adhesion, 69
agitation, 35
air
    pockets, 42
    pressure, 39
animals, rolled snow, 69
apple bobbing, 15
aqueducts, 8
arch, 8
aroma, 77
atmosphere, 78
atmospheric pressure, 39
atoms, 38
barometer, 39
bean sprouts, 29
bent beam, 22
beverage, iced, 72
bleeding, 54
blending, 37
blots, water, 53
boating, safety, 79
brittleness, 63
building blocks, 70
bulging water, 13
buoyancy, 15, 43
capillarity, 55
capillary action, 55
celery, tinted, 55
chimes, glass, 21
cisterns, 8
clock, water, 45
cohesion, 13, 14
color spectrum, 75
compacting, 70
compression, 70
condensation, 72
conduits, 49
creeks, 32
crops, irrigating, 7
croutons, 78
crystals, ice, 33, 58, 67, 68
currents, 41
density, 20
depression, 36
dew, 72
dewdrops, 67
dispersion, 16
displacement, 15, 24, 43

dissolving, 37
diversion, 49
dripping, 45
droplet painting, 46
droplets, 38
egg, submarine, 20
emulsion, 38
energy, 52
erosion, 49
evaporation, 56, 65, 78
expansion, 59
fishbowl, painted, 30
floating, 14, 15
flow, 12, 47
fluidity, 47
formations, 64
formula, chemical, 10
fractures, 63
fragrance, 77
freezing, 59–60, 64
    rate, 65
frost, 67
fruit, blow-up, 27
game in a jar, 41
garden
    rainbow, 18
    windowsill, 28
gas, 10, 58
geotropism, 29
germination, 29
glaciers, 70
glass
    chimes, 21
    magnifying, 23
gravity, 34, 39
habitat, 30
haunted house, 76
heat, 40
heat energy, 65
heliotropism, 29
H₂O, 10; *see also* water
"holes" in water, 16
horizon, 34
hothouse, 73
humidity, 72
hydrotropism, 29
ice, punch, 60
ice, safety on, 79
icebergs, 63
ice cream, 66
ice crystals, 67, 68

ice floes, 63
icicles, 64
igloos, 70
inclusions, 60
irrigation, 7, 49
Jack Frost, 67
lakes, 12
leaching, 17
leap frog, 50
level, 34
light waves, 22
liquid, 10, 12, 33
magic
    disappearance, 42
    floats, 14
magnification, 23
magnifying glass, 23
marbleized eggs, 26
matter, 10
meander pattern, 49
melting, 61
mist, 74, 75
molding, 70
molecules, 13, 14, 16, 40
oil paints, 54
overturn, 35
painted fishbowl, 30
paints, 54
people, early, and water, 7
pipes, water, 49
plants, thirsty, 56
pollution, 17
potpourri, simmering, 77
precipitation, 71
precipitation gauge, 71
preservation, 60
pressure, 38, 61
prism, 75
quill pen, 47
race, sailboat, 43
rainbow, 75
    garden, 18
raindrops, 45
rain gauge, 71
reconstitution, 27
recycling, 73
reflections, 44, 76
refraction, 22
refrigeration, 66
rejuvenation, 56

reservoirs, 12
ripples, 44
rivers, 32
rock(s)
    candy, 19
    sink like a, 24
    skipping, 44
roots, 28
safety, water, 79
sailboat race, 43
salt, 61
saturation, 19
sediment, 35
seepage, 26
separation, 38
sinking, 24, 25
siphoning, 50
"skin," 14
skipping rocks, 44
slide, water, 48
sliding, 62
smells, 77
snow animals, rolled, 69
snow cone, 63
snowflake catcher, 68
snow globe, 35
snow stick, 71
solid, 33
solution, 37
solvents, 18
sound, 21
spatters, 46
spectrum, color, 75
spoon, suspended, 74
spouts, water, 51
spreading, 53
springs, 8
stalactites, 45
stalagmites, 45
steam, 76
streams, 48
submarine egg, 20
suction, 50, 74
summer hockey, 62
sun tea, 17
surface tension, 14
suspended spoon, 74
suspension, 37
swimming, safety, 79
tart & sweet, 37
tea, sun, 17

tee-shirt, 54
tempera paints, 54
temperature, 25
terrarium, 73
thirsty plants, 56
transpiration, 73
travel, by water, 9
underwater eruption, 40
vacuum, 74
vapor, 33
vibrations, 44
volume, 71
vortex, 36
water
    beginnings, 6
    blots, 53
    bulging, 13
    characteristics, 10; *see also specific character-istics*
    clock, 45
    cycle of, 33
    defined, 10
    early people and, 7
    forms of, 58
    formula, chemical, 10
    growing, 59
    "holes" in, 16
    journey over land, 32
    management, 8
    molecule, 38
    pipes, 49
    pressure, 39, 51
    safety, 79
    slide, 48
    smarts, 79
    spouts, 51
    for travel, 9
    uses, 12
    wheel, 52
watercolor paints, 54
water-soluble paints, 46
weight, 51
wells, 8
wheel, water, 52
whirlpool, 36
whirlwind, 36
windowsill garden, 28